EMMANUEL JOSEPH

From Fiat to Bitcoin: Transforming the Trade Landscape

Copyright © 2025 by Emmanuel Joseph

All rights reserved. No part of this publication may be reproduced, stored or transmitted in any form or by any means, electronic, mechanical, photocopying, recording, scanning, or otherwise without written permission from the publisher. It is illegal to copy this book, post it to a website, or distribute it by any other means without permission.

First edition

This book was professionally typeset on Reedsy.
Find out more at reedsy.com

Contents

1	Chapter 1	1
2	Chapter 1: The Rise of Digital Currency	2
3	Chapter 2: Understanding Blockchain Technology	4
4	Chapter 3: The Evolution of Trade and Currency	6
5	Chapter 4: The Mechanics of Bitcoin Transactions	8
6	Chapter 6: Integrating Bitcoin into the Global Economy	11
7	Chapter 7: The Future of Digital Payments	13
8	Chapter 8: Challenges and Risks in the Crypto Space	15
9	Chapter 9: The Impact of Bitcoin on Global Trade	17
10	Chapter 10: The Role of Altcoins in the Digital Economy	19
11	Chapter 11: The Environmental Impact of Bitcoin Mining	21
12	Chapter 12: Embracing the Future of Digital Trade	23

Chapter 1

From Fiat to Bitcoin: Transforming the Trade Landscape

Chapter 1: The Rise of Digital Currency

The journey from traditional fiat currencies to digital assets like Bitcoin has been nothing short of revolutionary. Initially dismissed by many as a passing fad, Bitcoin has grown into a significant force in the global financial landscape. This chapter delves into the origins of Bitcoin, tracing its roots back to the enigmatic figure Satoshi Nakamoto, who released the Bitcoin whitepaper in 2008. The invention of blockchain technology as the underlying framework for Bitcoin has provided a transparent, decentralized ledger system that has reshaped our understanding of currency and trade.

Bitcoin's rise has been fueled by its promise of decentralization, security, and lower transaction costs. Unlike traditional currencies, which are controlled by central banks and subject to monetary policies, Bitcoin operates on a peer-to-peer network, free from central authority. This decentralization has made it an attractive alternative for those seeking financial sovereignty and protection against inflation. In this chapter, we explore the key milestones in Bitcoin's history, from its early adoption by tech enthusiasts to its recognition as a legitimate financial instrument by institutional investors.

The chapter also examines the economic and social factors that have contributed to the growing acceptance of Bitcoin. As global markets become increasingly interconnected, the demand for a borderless, digital currency has intensified. Bitcoin offers a solution to the limitations of traditional fiat currencies, providing a means of exchange that transcends national boundaries and operates outside the conventional banking system. This chapter highlights the role of technology in driving this transformation and the potential implications for global trade.

Finally, this chapter sets the stage for the subsequent exploration of the broader digital currency ecosystem. Bitcoin's success has paved the way for the development of thousands of other cryptocurrencies, each with its unique features and use cases. By understanding the rise of Bitcoin, readers will gain a foundation for exploring the diverse world of digital assets and their impact on the future of trade.

3

Chapter 2: Understanding Blockchain Technology

At the heart of Bitcoin and other cryptocurrencies lies blockchain technology, a revolutionary system that has redefined how we think about data and transactions. This chapter provides an in-depth explanation of blockchain technology, breaking down its components and principles in a way that is accessible to readers without a technical background. By understanding blockchain, readers can appreciate the innovation that has enabled the rise of digital currencies.

Blockchain is essentially a decentralized, distributed ledger that records transactions across a network of computers. Each block in the chain contains a list of transactions, and once a block is added, it cannot be altered, ensuring the integrity and transparency of the data. This chapter explains the concept of decentralization and how it eliminates the need for intermediaries, such as banks, in financial transactions. The peer-to-peer nature of blockchain allows for direct transfers of value between parties, reducing costs and increasing efficiency.

The chapter also explores the various consensus mechanisms used in blockchain networks to validate transactions and maintain the integrity of the ledger. Proof of Work (PoW), the mechanism used by Bitcoin, and Proof of Stake (PoS), used by many other cryptocurrencies, are discussed in detail. By understanding these mechanisms, readers can grasp how blockchain ensures security and trust in a decentralized system.

Additionally, this chapter highlights the diverse applications of blockchain technology beyond cryptocurrencies. From supply chain management to voting systems, blockchain has the potential to revolutionize various industries by providing a secure, transparent, and tamper-proof method of recording transactions. By the end of this chapter, readers will have a solid understanding of blockchain technology and its far-reaching implications for trade and beyond.

4

Chapter 3: The Evolution of Trade and Currency

Trade and currency have evolved significantly over the centuries, from bartering systems to the complex financial instruments we use today. This chapter traces the history of trade and currency, highlighting key developments that have shaped our modern economic landscape. By understanding this historical context, readers can better appreciate the transformative impact of digital currencies like Bitcoin.

The chapter begins with an exploration of early bartering systems, where goods and services were exchanged directly. As societies grew more complex, the limitations of bartering led to the development of commodity money, such as gold and silver, which had intrinsic value and were widely accepted as a medium of exchange. This chapter discusses the role of precious metals in facilitating trade and the eventual transition to paper money backed by these commodities.

The introduction of fiat currencies marked a significant shift in the history of trade and currency. Unlike commodity money, fiat currencies have no intrinsic value and are backed solely by the trust in the issuing government. This chapter explores the rise of fiat currencies, their impact on global trade, and the challenges they have faced, such as inflation and currency devaluation. By understanding these challenges, readers can see the potential advantages of digital currencies in providing a stable and decentralized alternative.

Finally, this chapter sets the stage for the transition to digital currencies by examining the role of technology in modernizing trade and finance. The advent of the internet and advancements in cryptography have enabled the development of digital payment systems and cryptocurrencies. By tracing the evolution of trade and currency, readers will gain a deeper understanding of the factors driving the shift from fiat to Bitcoin and other digital assets.

5

Chapter 4: The Mechanics of Bitcoin Transactions

Understanding how Bitcoin transactions work is crucial for anyone looking to navigate the world of digital currencies. This chapter provides a detailed explanation of the mechanics of Bitcoin transactions, from the creation of a Bitcoin wallet to the confirmation of transactions on the blockchain. By mastering these concepts, readers can confidently engage in Bitcoin transactions and appreciate the technology's innovation.

Bitcoin transactions begin with the creation of a digital wallet, which serves as a secure storage for Bitcoin and other cryptocurrencies. This chapter explains the different types of wallets, including software, hardware, and paper wallets, and their respective security features. Readers will learn how to create and manage a wallet, as well as best practices for keeping their assets safe.

The chapter also delves into the process of sending and receiving Bitcoin. Each transaction involves a transfer of value from one wallet address to another, with the details recorded on the blockchain. This chapter explains the components of a Bitcoin transaction, including inputs, outputs, and transaction fees. By understanding these elements, readers can better navigate the process and avoid common pitfalls.

CHAPTER 4: THE MECHANICS OF BITCOIN TRANSACTIONS

Additionally, this chapter covers the role of miners in validating and confirming Bitcoin transactions. Miners use computational power to solve complex mathematical puzzles, securing the network and adding new transactions to the blockchain. This chapter explains the concept of mining, the incentives for miners, and the impact of mining on the overall security and stability of the Bitcoin network.

By the end of this chapter, readers will have a comprehensive understanding of how Bitcoin transactions work and the underlying technology that makes them possible. This knowledge is essential for anyone looking to participate in the growing ecosystem of digital currencies and leverage the benefits of decentralized finance.

Chapter 5: Bitcoin vs. Traditional Banking

The advent of Bitcoin has sparked intense debate about the future of traditional banking. This chapter compares the key differences between Bitcoin and conventional banking systems, highlighting the strengths and weaknesses of each. By understanding these distinctions, readers can appreciate the transformative potential of Bitcoin and other cryptocurrencies.

One of the most significant differences between Bitcoin and traditional banking is the level of decentralization. While banks operate under centralized authority and regulatory oversight, Bitcoin functions on a decentralized network, free from government control. This chapter explores the implications of decentralization for financial autonomy, security, and transparency. By eliminating intermediaries, Bitcoin offers a more direct and cost-effective way to transfer value.

Another key distinction lies in the accessibility of financial services. Traditional banks often have stringent requirements for account opening and impose fees for various services. Bitcoin, on the other hand, provides an open and inclusive financial system that anyone with an internet connection can access. This chapter discusses the potential of Bitcoin to promote financial inclusion, particularly in regions with limited banking infrastructure.

The chapter also examines the differences in transaction speed and cost. While traditional bank transfers can take days and incur high fees, Bitcoin transactions are typically faster and cheaper. This chapter analyzes the factors contributing to these differences, such as network congestion and transaction fees. By understanding these factors, readers can better assess the advantages and challenges of using Bitcoin for everyday transactions.

6

Chapter 6: Integrating Bitcoin into the Global Economy

As Bitcoin gains mainstream acceptance, its integration into the global economy is becoming increasingly important. This chapter explores the various ways Bitcoin is being adopted by businesses, governments, and individuals worldwide. By examining real-world use cases, readers can gain insights into the practical applications of Bitcoin and its potential impact on the global economy.

One of the most notable areas of Bitcoin adoption is in cross-border payments. Traditional remittance services often involve high fees and lengthy processing times. Bitcoin offers a faster and more cost-effective alternative, enabling seamless cross-border transfers. This chapter provides examples of companies and platforms leveraging Bitcoin for remittances and explores the benefits and challenges of this use case.

Bitcoin is also being integrated into e-commerce and retail. Many businesses now accept Bitcoin as a payment method, providing customers with more payment options and enhancing the shopping experience. This chapter discusses the advantages of accepting Bitcoin for merchants, such as lower transaction fees and reduced risk of chargebacks. By understanding these benefits, readers can see the potential for Bitcoin to transform the retail landscape.

Governments are also exploring the use of Bitcoin and blockchain technology to enhance public services and improve efficiency. This chapter highlights examples of government initiatives involving Bitcoin, such as digital identity verification and transparent record-keeping. By examining these initiatives, readers can appreciate the broader implications of Bitcoin adoption for governance and public administration.

7

Chapter 7: The Future of Digital Payments

Digital payments are rapidly evolving, with Bitcoin and other cryptocurrencies at the forefront of this transformation. This chapter explores the future of digital payments, examining the trends and innovations shaping the landscape. By understanding these developments, readers can better navigate the changing financial ecosystem and capitalize on emerging opportunities.

One of the key trends in digital payments is the rise of mobile payment solutions. With the proliferation of smartphones, mobile wallets and payment apps have become increasingly popular. This chapter discusses how Bitcoin is being integrated into mobile payment systems, enabling users to make seamless transactions using their smartphones. By embracing mobile payments, Bitcoin can reach a broader audience and drive further adoption.

Another trend is the development of stablecoins, which combine the benefits of digital currencies with the stability of fiat currencies. Stablecoins aim to address the volatility of cryptocurrencies, making them more suitable for everyday transactions. This chapter explores the role of stablecoins in the future of digital payments and their potential to bridge the gap between traditional finance and the crypto world.

Additionally, the chapter examines the impact of decentralized finance (DeFi) on digital payments. DeFi platforms offer innovative financial services, such as lending, borrowing, and yield farming, without intermediaries. This chapter discusses how DeFi is transforming digital payments and providing users with greater financial autonomy and flexibility.

8

Chapter 8: Challenges and Risks in the Crypto Space

While the potential of Bitcoin and other cryptocurrencies is immense, there are also significant challenges and risks that must be addressed. This chapter provides an in-depth analysis of the key challenges facing the crypto space, from regulatory uncertainty to security vulnerabilities. By understanding these risks, readers can make informed decisions and mitigate potential pitfalls.

Regulatory uncertainty is one of the most pressing challenges in the crypto space. Governments worldwide are grappling with how to regulate digital currencies, resulting in a patchwork of laws and regulations. This chapter explores the regulatory landscape for cryptocurrencies, examining the approaches taken by different countries and the potential impact on the industry. By staying informed about regulatory developments, readers can navigate the legal complexities of the crypto space.

Security is another critical concern for cryptocurrency users. While blockchain technology itself is secure, the platforms and services built on top of it can be vulnerable to hacks and breaches. This chapter discusses the common security risks in the crypto space, such as phishing attacks, malware, and exchange hacks. By following best practices for security, readers can protect their digital assets and minimize the risk of loss.

The chapter also addresses the challenges of scalability and transaction speed. As the popularity of cryptocurrencies grows, the demand on blockchain networks increases, leading to congestion and higher fees. This chapter explores the various solutions being developed to address these scalability issues, such as layer 2 protocols and sharding. By understanding these solutions, readers can better assess the future viability of different cryptocurrencies.

9

Chapter 9: The Impact of Bitcoin on Global Trade

Bitcoin's influence on global trade is undeniable. This chapter explores how Bitcoin is reshaping international commerce by offering a decentralized, borderless means of exchange. By understanding the impact of Bitcoin on global trade, readers can appreciate its potential to revolutionize the way businesses operate across borders.

One of the key benefits of Bitcoin in global trade is the reduction of transaction costs. Traditional cross-border payments often involve multiple intermediaries, each charging fees that can add up significantly. Bitcoin transactions, on the other hand, are peer-to-peer and typically incur lower fees. This chapter discusses how businesses can leverage Bitcoin to reduce costs and improve their bottom line.

Bitcoin also offers increased transparency and security for international trade. The blockchain's immutable ledger ensures that all transactions are recorded and cannot be tampered with, reducing the risk of fraud. This chapter explores the potential of blockchain technology to enhance supply chain transparency and traceability. By implementing blockchain, businesses can improve trust and efficiency in their supply chains.

Additionally, Bitcoin's global nature allows for seamless transactions across borders, bypassing the limitations of traditional banking systems.

This chapter examines real-world examples of businesses using Bitcoin for international trade, highlighting the benefits and challenges they face. By understanding these case studies, readers can gain insights into the practical applications of Bitcoin in global commerce.

10

Chapter 10: The Role of Altcoins in the Digital Economy

While Bitcoin remains the most well-known cryptocurrency, thousands of other digital assets, known as altcoins, have emerged, each with unique features and use cases. This chapter explores the role of altcoins in the digital economy and their potential to complement Bitcoin. By understanding altcoins, readers can diversify their portfolios and explore new opportunities in the crypto space.

Altcoins, such as Ethereum, Litecoin, and Ripple, offer various functionalities beyond Bitcoin's store of value and medium of exchange. Ethereum, for example, introduced smart contracts, enabling decentralized applications (dApps) and programmable transactions. This chapter discusses the innovative use cases of prominent altcoins and their impact on the broader digital economy.

The chapter also examines the role of stablecoins, which are designed to maintain a stable value by being pegged to fiat currencies. Stablecoins offer the benefits of cryptocurrencies, such as fast and low-cost transactions, while minimizing volatility. This chapter explores the potential of stablecoins to bridge the gap between traditional finance and the crypto world, providing a stable medium of exchange and store of value.

Additionally, this chapter highlights the importance of conducting thorough research before investing in altcoins. With thousands of cryptocurrencies available, identifying promising projects requires careful evaluation of their technology, team, and market potential. By understanding the diverse landscape of altcoins, readers can make informed investment decisions and capitalize on emerging trends.

11

Chapter 11: The Environmental Impact of Bitcoin Mining

Bitcoin mining, the process by which new bitcoins are created and transactions are validated, has significant environmental implications. This chapter examines the environmental impact of Bitcoin mining, exploring the concerns surrounding its energy consumption and potential solutions for sustainable mining practices. By understanding these issues, readers can make informed decisions and contribute to the development of a more sustainable crypto ecosystem.

Bitcoin mining requires substantial computational power, leading to high energy consumption. This chapter discusses the factors contributing to Bitcoin's energy-intensive nature, such as the Proof of Work (PoW) consensus mechanism and the increasing difficulty of mining puzzles. By understanding these factors, readers can grasp the environmental challenges associated with Bitcoin mining.

The chapter also explores the geographic distribution of mining operations and their environmental impact. Many mining facilities are located in regions with abundant and inexpensive energy sources, such as hydropower. However, concerns have been raised about the reliance on non-renewable energy sources, such as coal, in some areas. This chapter examines the environmental consequences of different energy sources and their implications for Bitcoin mining.

To address these concerns, various initiatives and solutions are being developed to promote sustainable mining practices. This chapter discusses the potential of renewable energy sources, such as solar and wind, to power mining operations. Additionally, innovations like Proof of Stake (PoS) and other energy-efficient consensus mechanisms are explored as alternatives to PoW. By understanding these solutions, readers can appreciate the efforts to mitigate the environmental impact of Bitcoin mining.

12

Chapter 12: Embracing the Future of Digital Trade

The future of trade is digital, and Bitcoin is at the forefront of this transformation. This chapter looks ahead to the future of digital trade, examining the trends and innovations that will shape the landscape. By embracing these developments, readers can position themselves for success in the evolving digital economy.

One of the key trends shaping the future of digital trade is the increasing adoption of blockchain technology across various industries. From supply chain management to healthcare, blockchain has the potential to revolutionize the way we conduct business. This chapter discusses the potential applications of blockchain technology and how it can enhance transparency, security, and efficiency in trade.

Another trend is the rise of decentralized finance (DeFi), which offers innovative financial services without intermediaries. DeFi platforms enable users to lend, borrow, and trade digital assets seamlessly. This chapter explores the potential of DeFi to democratize finance and provide greater financial autonomy. By understanding the implications of DeFi, readers can leverage these platforms to enhance their trading strategies.

The chapter also examines the role of non-fungible tokens (NFTs) in the digital economy. NFTs represent unique digital assets and have gained significant attention in art, gaming, and entertainment. This chapter discusses the potential of NFTs to create new economic opportunities and reshape various industries. By understanding the impact of NFTs, readers can explore new avenues for innovation and investment.

Finally, this chapter emphasizes the importance of continuous learning and staying informed about the latest developments in the crypto space. The digital economy is dynamic and rapidly evolving, and staying ahead requires constant adaptation. By embracing new technologies and trends, readers can thrive in the future of digital trade and contribute to the ongoing transformation.

SUMMARY

In a world increasingly driven by digital innovation, **"From Fiat to Bitcoin: Transforming the Trade Landscape"** offers a comprehensive guide to understanding the profound shifts happening in global trade and finance. This book takes readers on a journey from the traditional world of fiat currencies to the revolutionary impact of Bitcoin and blockchain technology.

Starting with the origins of Bitcoin and the principles of blockchain, the book provides a solid foundation for those new to the world of digital currencies. It traces the evolution of trade and currency, highlighting the pivotal moments that have shaped our current financial systems. The book then delves into the mechanics of Bitcoin transactions, comparing them with traditional banking and exploring the benefits and challenges of integrating Bitcoin into the global economy.

Readers will gain insights into the broader digital currency ecosystem, including the role of altcoins, the rise of decentralized finance (DeFi), and the environmental impact of Bitcoin mining. The book also addresses the critical issues of security, regulatory challenges, and the future of digital payments.

By the end of this journey, readers will have a thorough understanding of the transformative potential of Bitcoin and other digital assets. **"From Fiat to Bitcoin: Transforming the Trade Landscape"** is an essential read for anyone looking to navigate the rapidly changing world of digital finance and trade.

www.ingramcontent.com/pod-product-compliance
Lightning Source LLC
LaVergne TN
LVHW020743090526
838202LV00057BA/6201